3.14159+

Lois Hirshkowitz

2004

3.14159+

BARROW STREET PRESS

New York City

For information about permission to reproduce selections from this book, write to:
Barrow Street Press, P.O. Box 1831, Murray Hill Station, New York, NY 10156.

Library of Congress Cataloging-in-Publication Data

Hirshkowitz, Lois
3.14159+ : poems / Lois Hirshkowitz
cm.
ISBN 0-9728302-2-7
I. Title
PS –2004

Grateful acknowledgment is made to the editors of the following publications in which these poems or versions of these poems first appeared: *American Letters & Commentary, Art/Life, CrazyHorse, First Intensity, LUCID MOON, The Journal, Poetry in Performance, The Paris Review, Prosodia, Salonika Quarterly, The Manhattan Review, tight, yefief.*

Thank you to all who have guided and nurtured this poet and these poems: *Patricia Carlin, Peter Covino, Melissa Hotchkiss, Evelyn Reilly, Ron Drummond, Walter Holland, Brenda Hillman, Robert Hass,* and *Elaine Equi.* A special thanks to *Molly Peacock* for her help and encouragement.

Also by Lois Hirshkowitz

Nurture & Torture
Marking Her Questions
Pan's Daughters

for Archie

            Matter,
energy, the speed of light: the universe
can be explained by an equation. Everything
that goes from one side of the equal sign
is exactly replaced from the other; i.e.,
nothing much happens at a speed so fast
we scarcely notice it, but so steadily
the math always checks out. This is thought
as I know and love it.
                              —*William Matthews*

three

point

one

three

OF MENTAL IMAGES THAT ARE UNUSUALLY VIVID
AND ALMOST PHOTOGRAPHICALLY EXACT OR
THROUGH THE EYES OF A BEETLE

Three large projections appear on the walls of a completely dark
room

She hears a whack-whack and thinks a loose shutter

Wind drawing open a curtain of fog plunges her
Into a threshold barely visible

At random intervals forms first bathed then consumed in light
Fill the field of indecipherable noise

The water she'll squeeze from this spongy world
Pools at her feet

Moving under a glass ceiling into the rippling
She stares at a man's face quietly whispering *it's stopping*

Only the lingering drips
Now letting

The eidetic spin a while longer
Pulling her in and out and out

I.

In the one photo, the one on the wall on the left, she knows she knew one of them well, knows how she took the pins out, but the man standing beside her is the stranger who died eight months before she was born so he could give his name to her and then, when she was old enough, his bed and dresser, and the big mirror that hangs over it where she pretends that he at least knows enough English to tell her the stories her own father (he thought she wasn't interested) told to her son, but not to her.

2.

Humoresque

3.

Above her computer hang two she talks to every day, her mother must have told her their names but 1943 is so long ago and how's a seven-year-old to remember things like that, and after a while her mother couldn't say their names or the names of all the others, her whole family, all in Warsaw playing hide-and-seek, all at the wrong time, and looking at them now, she notices her aunt wore frameless glasses held on only at the bridge of her nose and here's an idea, her own earpieces are always hurting her, and that's when she pronounces

4.

Sonia
Eliezer

5.

Is it more or less sensible to sleep this morning that the sky is white against the tops of the buildings, yes even the Chrysler Building is blacker than she has ever seen it, that she, in trying to capture that white closes her eyes only to find other colors intruding into it, red for example, for the red she knows the light has turned, it was so still for a few seconds, and green now, for now the traffic in its liquid way, how she loves to use water words, whooshing, flowing, streaming, and then used to the sounds she lets herself see grays, why gray, you ask, replays *Tape* and *Further than the Furthest Point*, the shades of dark gray and black in the one bleak motel, black in the other because wasn't it true that in both plays people suddenly knew that they didn't and who did, she doesn't, but shouldn't she finally go downstairs to her desk and look at the walls lined with the photos of family and shouldn't she face them, yes, say it, she was frightened that one day soon someone would look into her eyes and say, "I wonder who she was."

6.

They are the   who(?) were they   here (they) watch:

Afterwards, a would-be picture postcard
Near patches of water her shirt will shed

Two, no three, in a blur building their nest

Her shirt well retted and scotched
One sleeve draped across the other over the arm

There's the line she wouldn't cross
She looks at the picture through a mirror, missing lots of the
words
She wonders if she will lose her senses one by one in this scene

The light is so soft and ambiguous it's hard to hear

Imagining it, she shuts the light door of her dreams
Where she had been acting for an audience
Imagines that from now they will act only for each other

He'll tell her exactly what he wants her to say
Tomorrow or Thursday, she could say

In this dream she's the escort for the man
Who has been her husband for thirty-eight years
In his search for a new wife
He needs her advice
He's narrowed it down to three
Which one?

The first dream told her she has a lump
Below her ear that only comes out at night
She starts to cry, *Why didn't I notice it?*
She moves it easily, names it moonflower
No, that's not a good name
No, this will not do at all
There's nothing to laugh at here

She drinks an entire glass of water
The lineup out the door and around the block
She'd better speed up the interviews

Next!
She takes another sip and
Isn't there anyone out there
Who wants to make *her* laugh?
Where is everyone?
The window transforms
A door slams
Get
Up Get

Rock a bye shadows drumming a grim tattoo on the tree trunk
Arrhythmic play of children chattering in wind twist and twine

That morning the honking of horns tried to
On this one a garbage truck
Backing up tried, too
And then the three hammer blows

And there it is: on this one not so cold and crisp morning she
finds herself
De-centering (she's grown shell *and* wings)
Aging more slowly, not dying yet
Breathes when she says *breathe*
She is   *I am*

Some of the trees here are three hundred years old
And still putting out

Drives her car into

        A smooth scream

Flat low sheets of light

        The gift from you

Down the long hallway

        Turning the wheel

Makes the right turn

        That turns me into

Leaves the back way

        Afteryouafteryouafteryou

Travels on back roads

        Watching the evening dance of the bee

No lights to slow her

        Knowing the sound of its being

A long line of old men walks single file
On the up slope of the wall down the hallway
Skin stretched over bare bones
Cheeks shiny
Protruding
Down and up and across
The charms on my bracelet
Across the carpet squares lining up for the parade
The line stretching
To the end of the street

Why did I think "of" old men?
His stooped shoulders following
His, his trail becoming circle
Circle getting smaller
Encircling me

The ground under the dirt/dust on the floor vibrating

Shaking my hand as I write "write"
My hand afraid that I'm not afraid
In this day's grid
And it will take three scruples
To push the spirit back in

Watching a pantomime

Feeling this push-pulling every night since her two
old folks passed

The baby sparrow caught between glass and screen

Beating and b-b-beating against the window

Then, on mute and rewinding

One by one the figures, hidden beneath a large,
black cloth, enter

Sees herself as a woman in her late forties in an elegant gown,
trying to sit down

Then as a palpable flutter

Then shoulder to shoulder in a circle, locked in

Her right hand on her mother's right shoulder, it's bare,
her father's hand in hers

And so on

Can't see who completes the circle

Slide-step slide-step slide-step JUMP
slide-step slide-step slide-step JUMP

Need to work on JUMP, not yet, not yet

appeared on the lot one morning last week
and wouldn't leave

a pretty old white car
Monday morning or Tuesday last week

might have been Monday
I thought on my way home

didn't the lot look empty before
it and its front right flat

Whose is it?
Of course it's his, the boy who showed up

in the middle of the night I dreamed my mother
was dying again and my very old (but alive)

father wouldn't stop crying and
I'm handing him tissue after tissue

The next day the lot looked like the lot
without it and them

Sometimes what someone says sounds like the language
children in a room by themselves will invent.

Invent a word that gets lured into a place it wasn't trying to
get to—not much room in there for thinking.

Think: begin to, to end, all in the same second. Going over in
her mind what did that mean?

Meaning its sound and timing stun her, meaning three sharp
retorts in a thicket of dissonance: one couple stands up
and runs for the exit.

Exits through an elongated door frame.

Framed, unruly woman, arms akimbo, breasts swaying,
elbows raised, hair streaming and swooping, the last end of
anything she can remember.

Remember.

Remembered.

Remembers above the sea, the clouds and the light-glint in
a tug-of-war.

A woman wakes up
>someone took the conference table out of her office last night
>and near that tooth she's tender again
>she's grinding again

The woman waking up
>sees the ropes snap
>thinks suspenders *and* garter belts
>says *I've ground it down*

Waking up to drilling and scraping
>the whole building an oral cavity
>the dentist a team of masons
>pointing bricks
>ropes shake
>scaffolding at the open window

A woman up and down in her kitchen
>a carpenter playing the flute
>now in slow motion
>outside the kitchen window

When she wakes up she thinks no table so what
>weak light falling through air
>dense with old pulp
>and she thinks, waking up—ground down

How multitudinous of her   two of her here
Seeing herself on the screen in Alice Tully Hall
She closed her eyes that day
Looked up at herself in Brobdingnagian
Liked looking up seeing herself do it
Seeing to her inner proportions and to the others around her
Her self sticking out of the others around her looking up
And on the screen all in a shower of the purple
She sees as she feels herself getting hard
She *should* wear purple more often   look
How she is a burst of pleasure *allegro energico*
A technological bull's-eye: *molto allegro*
A Lilliputian at heart and proud to be
She should stand now

Now in the moment when her days are shorter
And nights cooler she knows it is time
Takes three of the apples sitting on the counter
Drops them with cinnamon bark and roasted
Sesame seeds into onions cooked in wine
Lets them simmer   will wait it out
She's getting better and better at simmer
Decides not to stir or churn or scrape
Sweets that stick to the bottom
The slices still look like sliced apple
The onion, onion   Good
At a slow boil this argument has whatever it needs
For resolution: each of the ingredients
Needing to hold the mixture together

1. The child sits on the beach thinking it will be green inside as she builds with her pail and smooths with her shovel that leaves indentations where she doesn't want them because these lines define spaces that don't want to be limited yet and shouldn't ever be, her mother writes as she writes, this child is in both of us, we're both building and smoothing but only when the tide is out and we're the only family still on the beach when the sun is behind us in the west waiting for us to go before it drops below the bay where the boats are coming after dropping hopeful lines and well-constructed nets into water where the fish don't stand a chance, one reason the two of them will be vegetarians when the child turns fourteen and her mother is 29 years older than she is and will be for the rest of their lives.

2. The last few days the air has been wetter over the Raritan River and what color and here's the fog that the sky-blue BMW needs to invade to get from there to there and I need to pull my jacket up from the seat and up over my shoulders and he needs to fiddle with the heat lever until a thinly heated air pushes its way through the mesh of ducts and up inside of the windows and look, we laugh, we are making a fog in here that I can spell into but I whisper "what isn't it?" and by the time we stop and I say the "when will we?" even "the" will want to feel what the damp is hiding under my tongue.

3. Always green, the interior is always green as soon as dark falls around her, whether her eyes are closed or not, green bedroom after bedroom, and from any of these bedrooms she can see into a room she will call the living room, for what else to call it, the passing room, the room-she-can-see-from-any-of-the-bedrooms she wanders through and although she and her daughter 23 years later are one, her startlingly beautiful face having replaced hers, but that's what she supposes: there are no mirrors in these rooms that the two-in-one pass through always passing never stopping or sitting the way the two of them sit on the beach as they construct each day each new home for them to wander into when the sun will fade into the bay where fish out-of-danger, finally, can feed and sleep.

point

Trying to dodge the cold jet just before the hot kicks in

One mother is not the same as another

The redwoods control all that is beneath them

A creature swallowed in shadows blows off steam

Show her the she's-tired-way to go home

The god dwelling in her car is different from the god dwelling in hers

One broken broken-promise is not the same as another

What is she doing here at the end of daylight saving time

At the boundary of where her where is hidden

Where a face is familiar on one side only

Where the fog disperses into a cloud of daylight

That swerves and swoops and crashes through her mirror

Into this little owl trying to hide that one at the top

One mother in a barn-like room   one's on the street

p.28//

one

And there it is all at once a red Russell Stover
Blimp flying north after the plane
That just took off from West Palm Beach
That takes so long to pass
First at the column's one side then to its other

Far away now the silver-coated almond
The sliver let out of a silk padded box
Swimming in the sky wings back breast protruding

Gives her a minute to inside it
Sitting there writing. inside in the sky's map
And, inside the nutty caramel strawberry creams

A lot of physics is going on here
Buoyancy and equality and all
That is and will be displaced

A camera tracks the pilgrim moving through the shrine
The pilgrim a little like a tile in the design
But wait the movie will open
A camera spying and
Dissolving into abandoned spaces
Frame-by-frame forgetting objects

Not a word is said not a note of music
This one-shot sequence single but continuous

Now a shell tree is rolling in the sand
Now a child-man depending on her caring
Now other women enter costumed and made up

In her dream she falls in love with a young man
And he with her caring
Not smiling he's looking straight ahead

He's telling me what he doesn't know
Doesn't know he'll say it
Before he's saying it
I know what he's saying

We all live downwind
Gleaming steel studs in stucco
Built for today's
Windowed and terraced to some bay

Tongue out
Blinded to what behinds us
Before this can be

The garbage stewing in the sun
And all I smell when the wind blows it my way
His sweetly laundered shirt

The day she hears her hands serenading her

My love   my you   my wife

she's only mildly surprised

finds her reflection in her left palm

playing itself out a half-inch from her finger

five beats to the measure

a tumble of events and you and you and

an oriental bittersweet at war with the cherry and winning

her red hair lighting the wall

the foxiness of it

her arms unfolding her

whispering   *from now on*

tonight a serenade only a serenade

she'll save her best dream for last

Sees the sun's lights meeting in paintbrushed clouds
Closes her eyes too much to know
Her camera isn't always from his point of view
A field an Ipomoea in a bossed mirror
Scratch mark wrinkles doesn't she see herself
Doesn't she want what she doesn't have to see
In the center of the white flower
Purple spokes stepping through the wall of a screen
And above her, her little egrets
Are scraps of paper with tails
Flirting this way and that way away
Clouds topping the sides of the crater
Mist her splicing the two together
The air sniffs her so

For tonight she's an opening
At *any* door

Tomorrow she'd like to be the one to
Rise against the yen or
Fall behind the mark

One wiggle then another
Then zip
The membrane bursting down the back
Gradually she'll be out of it

If she waits too long to ask
She may not be forgiven
And in front will be the white shore
The cliffs leaning on it

Someone else coaxes the youngest calf
Into and out of the water
Knowing its mother will follow
Herds rushing behind her
Lowing

And without a slip the calf will turn to *her* now
And now they are knee-knuckle in the water
Tongue-to-tongue deep in the surf
The cow and her calf

At 9:20 a.m. on the 59th anniversary of Pearl Harbor
My friend Rheba Gelbstein (born 11-11-11) died
Laughing at Charlotte Krupnick's joke about a "flucky."
A night or two later a spark flew into my eye
And when I woke into the pain
I woke into a dark, no-Rheba emptiness,
A cold space
How fitting
"What a pity," she would have said.

And wouldn't I have loved to tell her about parhelia:
The glare off the arctic ice that mimics a rainbow.

Wouldn't you think such beauty would stop
The pain of leaving her and now leaving this old house
Where lucky us, we found some peace,
The house where we had the three of them
Watched them
Then watched them go
Then come and go.

Today Jose Fuentes will come at noon
To collect the bedroom furniture he bargained for.
He and his wife will sleep on our bed on sheets
I laundered yesterday for them,
Baby Abigail and her big sister on our children's beds.

On this visit, Abigail, a sound-sparkler,
Will hold to walls and tables,
Will tease out giggles that grow inside her
Until they (if sounds can be in color, Rheba) will arc
And glow.

Seems fitting to begin in a room
Within a room within another room
On a steep slope
Covered with flat pieces of shale
Falling into a sky-high pile of folded clothes

Decides to keep the shades down
A spiderweb swaying in the breeze
That's how she knew it was going to be spring

But where is a place without grief?
Since this story is about the revelation of secrets
All of which did not alter the fact that
She should have stayed home
Fingers tip to tip about three or four of them at a time
And others waiting

The one who is waiting
And the one who is watching
A winding stair leading to a place
Inside now
Waiting out the words
She doesn't want to
Remember "afraid" and "being"
And "close" and
Disappear

(She knows she'll be sorry later)
Pulls out of the dark into a light light
A mauve morning feels how alone is
Except for the driver far away beeping
And the one who made him do it
That light that enters the frantic sleep that tries so
To hold on she knows it won't be back
There for a while in its narrative murk
Her body leaves its body the way the strings started after the beat
The way any bird would dart out of a tree
The way the superb starling left the acacia
Should she settle for what she'll see in the end?
(Knows if others know her story it isn't hers anymore)
What exactly does she want you to know? Everything?

For unexplained reasons a man wants to die
He will find someone surely he will
Won't he when he turns to you
And says, "You're on their side, aren't you?"
The hush will be huge and loud
Someone will cough and a child will wail
It will be impossible to say just where it began
And when it will end and when she remembers
The spine of zebra after zebra after zebra standing
Still and rock-silent against the gold of early evening
She is still in the moment before he'll decide to die
Her meeting is over there's nothing to do now
And more time to do it in even time to plan the evening
Yes she'll set it first and then she'll see

four

Saying the best days of my life
Haven't happened yet and
Coming and going do-si-do so
May be another delighting hatching

And love's secret unlocking where you and
Where two in(ter)sect go twice
As no end to it   so fast so what
The uplift   the promenade your partner

Now the circle right hand around
Each other each hand juddering and
"When you looked at a beautiful car
Were you thinking engine?"

Yet, love, another beautiful surprise
A great laughter hopping about
"Where *did* all your friends go?"
Circling left and to the

After the indigo bunting sang his way
From the bottom of the tree to the top
And there in the brightest sunlight
Sang and sang and sang

She began to suspect
There might be trouble ahead

Two by two
They flew
Inside the dark room
Without the benefit of diffraction of light
Without knowing what time it was
Or where time was taking them

She sat dreaming in a full moon corner of the world
Rehearsing and improvising her songs
And when that, too, stopped
Even before she stopped, she knew
Stopping had potential

A woman wonders
—Why can't I finish anything?

She keeps her equipment in a gray container
Of course, her tardiness is definitely her excuse for
Lately, one partner is too young and inexperienced,
For example:

You never know when you're going to be dumped on.

Ways to get him to turn it off, ways to get him to turn it on.

Speaking of the curvature of space-time:
Did you notice that it's taking a little longer?
What's your angle?

If a naked woman would jump out of the baked-cake
What could fly out of a pie? Two dozen blackbirds?

She still wakes up in the morning the same person.

Flying   at
Home   a cat
A Tisket A Tasket
A leaping lady

A green and yellow scatter rug
         I lost it my scatter pin
         What a scatterbrain
         And the don't-know-where-I-put-it
         Scatology is
         Such scary shit

[*hiss = cat*]?
She knows=where she put it

      Hissing c-a-t-t-i-n-g calling her
      Someone who believes singing
      Singing c-a-l-l-i-n-g cat is
      Someone's only pleasure

      Calling h-i-s-s-i-n-g scat
      Her songs calling her

Scatcat
Come back!

Speeding up the air
Moving past the wings
Providing more lift

And the door opened out to her
So lightly touched so surprised to see
Two women already inside the stall

A moment before she remembers the firethorn
Already loosing its reddest
And two *had been* stroking her

Green gleaming strand that was holding
Flying in her own wake
Wasn't it daring that she saw herself in this story

Swans have something of an image to maintain

I see to my right what you see to your left
Reflection-magic here in the car
I look at my window, you out yours
We click.

Synchronicity makes my head happy
We call each other at the same moment
Both busy
We'll try later

The gnarl in my hair this morning in the same spot
As the knot I touched in last night's dream
The wiggles and wobbles of our little planet
Yanking us this way and that

The unhurried skein of the interconnected's
Sinuous routine not spontaneous but not rehearsed

Although she suspects a tear in the narrative fabric
A sleight of hand
A fascinating excursus on the limitations of sync-sound
She gives herself no room for amnesia

She so wants to find out what happened
To the people in her other poems
That she visits an old dream
Stands at the bus stop that fits into the curve of the sidewalk

Walks again through underground caverns
Not unfriendly, this time

At times she hears them or their rapid footsteps
But cannot see them
Too much noise in the foreground

Looked down at four long black witch's hairs
Growing on your kneecap

Smoking because you want to
Because sooner or later when the sun has given up the fight
This morning won't trick *you* into thinking winter

Because when you were younger you were more careful
Standing on a bridge looking like a half-moon

Standing on your head
An upside-down arch
In Downward Dog

No one back there to back you up or stop you

Stopping slowly, his story is about you
But I'm not a dog, you growl, I'm your wife

A woman walks in and sits down at the table
Who knows her?
She doesn't look like anyone I know
She sits there for days and minutes later
Her back is still the back of a stranger
No, we don't know her
Isn't it Athena sitting there
Watching us leave
Who needs this place anyway

In the next booth a child
Says to her mommy
Do we know where we're going?

We walk them home through the park
Two men are waiting at the door
Don't, I say
But, she insists, *you know how hard it is to find good repairmen*

Halfway into Sir Edgar Elgar's *The Dream of Gerontius*, opus 38, libretto based on the poem by Cardinal John Henry Newman, performed without an intermission, the tenor, Anthony Dean Griffey, who holds degrees from Wingate University, the Eastman School of Music *and* the Juilliard School, has barely sung (*andante*)

> *Sanctus fortis, sanctus Deus*
> *De profundis, oro te*

when a man sitting deep in the orchestra, row M, gets up, falls down, and lies there, still.

> *Miserere, Judex meus*   Have mercy, my Judge
> *Mortis in discrimine*   In the critical moment of death

At once, one team of experts in the audience tries to revive him, another to calm the woman at his side. Inconsolable, she crawls in the aisle and row looking for his lost shoe.

> Rescue him, O Lord in this his evil hour

And then they arrive, the NYC emergency crew, and we see, and everyone else sitting above the man lying in the aisle near row M sees, he is breathing. Let the Westminster Symphonic Choir punch it out fortissimo

> Rescue him, O Lord

And let the priest, John Relyea, who began studying voice with his father, a renowned Canadian bass-baritone, announce

> *Proficiscere anima Christiane, de hoc mundo*
> Go forth upon thy journey, Christian soul

And as the two men in uniform wheel him (on a stretcher) out, let us say

> Amen

Sir Colin Davis conducted.

four

one

They said the women should go

She puts the Latin verb *exeo* into her mouth
Finds *exit* and *exeunt* and *egress* hiding
But "go" is hard on her tongue and glottis
Her incisors click *exitexit*

They need ten men in here
They said the women should go

She doesn't move
Sees the baby's legs are in a plastic harness
His penis standing up
From here a sharpened pencil
His screams the sharpener

His blood splattering from the mohel's mouth
Onto a napkin
Onto the white carpet
A drop or two into the *kiddush* cup

One or two too many he-s here
And where are all the she-s:
One on her knees cleaning the carpet
One directing
One filming
One watching
One crying the way home

What if energy does *not*   wait   sit   no

The sun   look there   harnessed muscle fibers

At fast twitch an accelerating lope

Touching ground how so many million times

A minute   consider this handful

This kaleidoscopic processor

A seeming menagerie of leads and pulls

An inside door to the storage room store

Sale: room-roaring   in-winds   up down whistles

A round one or more beats interlocking

Some in some more thing out of phase or less

Some where some this rock-a-buzz-a jumping

(Sit down here little scarlet locoweed)

Where no thing will put some every to sleep

Flying inside a lightbulb she sensed
An endless expanse of ice
Marked it down: *white horizon*
So when the plumber woke her to tell
Her, "I am on my way,"
The little girl playing the piano

Had already started shrinking and the piano
Addicted to playing and replaying sensed
It was the little girl's way
Into a frame within the frame of the ice-
White expanse, time to tell
Jupiter who's dominating the horizon's

Southeastern sky until daybreak when the horizon
Will turn ah! she'll be inside the piano
You're looking more telling
Here's where it squeaks, sensing
He's looking more and more, his long ice-
White hair loose on the pillow that way

But then the way Jupiter turned away
From her ah! falling into the horizon's
Ice-
Water, pulsating in time to the piano's
Strings that sensed
She would tell

The story but who would believe she was telling
It the way
It happened that night or the way she sensed
Horizon
Her body joined first inside the piano
And then inside the light's expanse of ice

Keying it down: *endless ice*
Telling
It on the piano
Playing it all ways
Until the horizon
Itself senses her ah!

And where are mother and father during all of this
Parents do play favorites

Which one of us is the insurance policy against accidents

I'm further in the ground than you are
And finally I like being

Like stewing in my own chemical juices
Plum puddings aren't inherently unstable

It occurs to me that a racetrack isn't quite the right metaphor
either

Too many other things are happening here
Inside this salad bowl of a hillscape
Wind indeed   a wooed mate wooing
My spider running off at the lip

Watch them all come and go and always out of reach
Lovely

In the day's half lights   *breathe   jump   breathe*
Breath   *jump*   now into time all in a breath
A single breath, the only breath left
The second time the breath comes back to her
Shouting   *jump*   the third time whispering   *I am*
On time   saying   *hear this*   and here this and her this
Before this time with time seconding the breath
As it is and as it will place her here
As here she forgets   *jump*
Forgets sliding away leaving
Its trail   undone itself deleting
One point for all her imperfect heroines
She falling down laughing saying   *slide*
Android, slide

1. He worries that someone cut his hair while he was asleep
    last night

2. She, that neither he nor she will last forever

3. And to top it off
    It is pouring
    And she, walking onto the train platform in Seattle
    Rain lashing out at her, wonders
    Where is 15th Avenue?
    A family going and coming huddles

1. This dreamless night is
    Making her tired and tired
    Must have
    Had to work
    Hard to stay asleep

1. *May I borrow your glasses?* She asks
    A woman sits at a desk

2. Laptop open and buzzing away

3. *Don't drop them*
    They'll scratch

1. Examining herself
    Screams (she's in the Ladies' Room at Port Authority)
    Look what's happened to you
    This breast was firm and high
    When you left the house this morning
    Bitch, look what you look like now

In unison she reaches in to touch
The canyon like a stairway
Her vibration at the rate of

Plunges into a slow sweeping glide
A solid sheet of water falling down the face
And in the key of now she sees
Breast puffed out and trilling

Needing an answer now she doesn't
Her self's melody is still inside
A patch of scarlet bee balm
The hummer who can't smell mud and mist

Blindfolded can't tell a robin from a wren
Sounds so simple match the song to the singer
Defacto hawk'll have to learn to hunt in the day

As small as an infant's fingernail
Rimmed by shadows of rain forest
In a sea nearly the temperature of blood
A dead leaf in a gentle surge
A she advertises with poster colors

A child who dreams
She is a Madame Alexander doll
Here the green table where she writes
I *am* going to get it
I'm going to get it

I can hear her yellows
Where she put what she didn't want anymore
The bureau she'd climb onto
After the keener screaked like a cat caught in the sheets
After the doorbell rang out: *Telegram!*

Finally after all these years
Writes it and in italics
Opens the door
Calls her
Her mother
Her mother comes to the door

No, a tumble dryer is not always the answer
After all, money does count: there are bathing suits
And precious sweaters pantyhose that need
An old fashioned drip over the bathtub
Or a spread over the bushes out back
Look, she sees stripes on the cool concrete floor
Is *that* today's password she amuses
What if today is a bad day for the dollar
What if he did say I look forward
Boy, do I look forward to my day in
And in the midst of August swoon at the market
She'll watch gargoyles dancing and the toothless singing
That day laundering, she knows, is back in town
And blue-ing here to turn tap water into the Caribbean

The fluorescent light of the first snowfall over Lake Carasaljo

Mondays' 6:30 a.m. sun in a corner of the rearview mirror
On the south side of the New Jersey Turnpike

What's sparkling on the crown of the Chrysler Building?

Watching 5 o'clock turn into a purple reflection
In the windows of the high-rise across the street

An orange shopping cart parked next to a black van under a
street lamp

And the yellow branches of the ginkgoes on East 35th

First look at top of the Walking Dunes in Montauk
Not too breathless not to gasp

Climbing back up for one more look at the dune heather
Seeing in the dark leaves a yellow-meadow promise

Two hooded red mergansers sunning out on glassy Napeague Bay

The slice of mica lying there on the beach
Holding it and putting it back in the sand

First his snoring
Then on the dock a dog barking
A motor boat coming closer
A terrace door rolling open
And I'm trying to be in the sound of the surf

And I'm trying to stay in the dream
Someone's embracing someone
Both in white and still
Too much into each other
I'm only the spectator walking
Towards

There *are* hillocks on the other side of the bay

Left the nail file on the table hoping that today
Finally I would get all ten
Quarter mooned
Perfect
No more no
Less but it doesn't pay to plan
Anymore after all and after all
There's that hearty breakfast
To look forward to
A lovely egg and crisp-edged

Down an empty street the curve of a low building
A turning car stops the traffic light jewel-bright

In the store's window the dancer in green motley
Waits for the piper to begin

And as you step off the curb something silver
Like a mechanical eel will pass

Elsewhere women mostly watched
Some were absent in conversations that keep

Cropping up again and again that don't
Have the juice to advance the story

five

Just as she sliced the last tomato
The knife pushing through
When the phone rang out, "Oh, no"
Tomato seeds lay in their own juice
The last slice ragged uneven

Putting her list in its place
She bends to count the seeds
Sits there wanting
Something else to arrive

Item: the boy who let the fish slide through his finger
Let it slip beneath the water's surface
And disappear. To her eyes, anyway

Item: energized by the blue crisp cliché of a day
A child bolts the hand that holds her
Joins a march-march into the reluctant circus
Not looking back at the hand
That held her
Inside the circle the dancers
Catch her march-march

Left? An unfurling gelatinous curtain?
Stinging tentacles gobbling up
The tomatoes the boy the blue crisp air
Her list in its own juice?

After words (one):
They asked her to play *America* with them
That's why she's humming it
They're all humming it these days
From C to shining

After words (five):
They rolled and touched as they swam away
Diving and surfacing in unison
Lingering.

1. A street I don't know is running down a man with igneous eyes.

2. The streetlight will go, too, and so soon dawn's soft, saturating light.

3. In this version, the man turned a corner, and the light is still dark. In this version he's the one who at the last minute would have turned them, turned them back.

4. E. will write a poem about her street—who's afraid and who will be.

5. Scraps of paper, food, feces—some still wet from yesterday's persistent drizzle—one paper-piece follows the street, falls and gets up.

6. Why is the night doorman reaching for his broom, 15 minutes to go before he goes, raindrops, an eerie interpolation to be swept inside the filamentous.

7. Inside an alarm that rings out, a light goes on. In the empty intersection, unfolding, a deftly elusive narrative.

8. If I can hear the time it takes trucks in the distance, I need to check my e-mail.

9. At around the same time, I sense it (I did not hear it at first): "Open the window." Some people just can't start talking.

10. A distant thunder-rumble. The fifth plane? What kind of man would disappear after dawn?

11. Bear in mind, someone may be tracking me down, eavesdropping. No, let's not put the cart there.

12. Close-up: A man in shorts walks by carrying a suit and a gym bag. I follow him. I sense I can ask, "Are you like me?"

13. The dumb and the deadly run, run for their lives.

Female finches go for males wearing red leggings

Will two promises go out the window when two strangers come in the door?

The contradiction is never resolved, and the finale leaves her

Neither home nor exiled gazing out at nothing

A woman's world ends

Fades to a chubby little girl topped by an explosion of frizzy hair

Weak light dense with old debris falls through the air

Nothing new can happen

She hears herself say

"I know you are very unhappy but I am more so."

How is she to find *more* so

When and if that little old man biodegrades

Later near the canal on the road

She goes into the last lock, and through

What if *how* she experiences
Is in the interval that defines the difference
Her reasons becoming   she reasons
About absence in this presenting of to be

For example: intertwined hands that almost touch each other

The price for consciousness is unconsciousness
Her brain seeing/hearing things that aren't there
The zebra that can tell when a lion is hungry for example
The monarch that will make the 2,000 mile round trip

A Möbius strip that never quite reaches closure

There is remarkable turbulence
Even on the quietest evening
Hard to see a reflection of river in the sky

But not impossible

Going to find Father

I go through a ward to get to the theater
Bald pasty sweet things lying still on the sheets
I peer over a balcony down into a room
Father is watching a screen
Showing someone peering down over his shoulder

There's nothing quite so beautiful he shouts to me
As a perfectly matched ball-and-socket joint
Nothing so graceful
As the slide of the radius
As it engineers the flick of the wrist
Nothing so smooth so white so cool
As the slope of the human hip

How does *he* know?

1. It will stop raining and everyone moves outside
    Two successive lightning streaks light up the dinner table
    And then faces turn inward again
    Where they may watch water acrobats
    From behind a glass wall

2. The mirrors are two feet tall from the floor up
    She sees chair legs and half legs crisscrossed
    Rearranged in a pancake-like cluster

3. From walk to march to skip to run
    To running with a skip
    To running with a skip while catching balls
    To running with a skip while catching balls connected to
    a bungee cord

4. Finally a dream!

    Staircases lead to staircases
    Steps to steps
    "K" to "L"
    "L" doesn't know where to go or when to stop

5. How perverse to want to be somewhere else
    Even when you are somewhat else

In that one   click-
      second   they are
        three: the child,

her sister,
and her sister's

      shadow   that covers
        half   the child
          up   against cold brick,

a wall   on Empire
corner   of Kingston

                  where   a pale outline
                  casts   a shadow.

    there's   the shadow

      in high   heeled pumps,
        one   foot poised,

her front hairs piled,
      dark lips apart.

      Under   the child's snug hat
      her hair
      hides

      for the moment.

i.

The moment before the moment
She falls asleep she hears
Her breath a transport from
The return trip that leaves
Something of her
But what

ii.

And what postmenopausal women aren't having babies now?
Which fat woman isn't skinny?

She's eating in the other room
Waiting for the action to start breaking down
Dust settles on the chest's vertical surface
And she's trying to get ready for the party

iii.

In the crevice of a boulder
A rubbery pink stem leads to
A mauve flower shaped
Like clover blossom

iv.

By mid night the curtain will start to dissolve
Her tatters her air shredded
Her patched air

v.

Hives on her arms
Her arms will turn blue from her scratching
Her daughter urges her to try herbal tea
Her husband a rich moisturizer
Tomorrow morning she'll bury them
Up to the elbow is as far as she'll go

What the viewer is left watching is
What's left out of the picture
The missing wristband
The roadway ending before the bridge
Once upon a time there was a mountain
Is the argument ever going to start
Is the car going to make it
And on the local news another building collapses
Two figures seen in long shot walking by
When it was still possible to do so
She, standing by the window
Staring at the bathrobe over her bare shoulders
A moment recorded at the moment she sees it
The five best mistakes she ever made, maybe

I'm last-page weird today the way Sundays are weird
The way a crumb would lodge itself in my throat
Little squares on a *Sunday-now* don't touch me the way
Now does on any other day
And let's suppose I can't turn the way
I do on any other page
The way I collect on this one
Wish I could slow the grid from filling
Saying I'll take my time drizzling down the sheet
(I do wish I hadn't said that, the street isn't wet yet)
The rainy season hasn't arrived yet
And could I ever make that wish that I were
(I'll bet there's someone out there)
Finally all out of words

Here this!

The male fruit fly evolved a seminal fluid so potent: not only was
it more effective at preventing the female from producing offspring
with any other male but it shortened her life.

To speak the name of the dead one is to give her life
Speak
What
Give
Give her

> Above the sea
> the clouds
> a quiet morning
> gentle breezes
> holy whispers

Rabbit is the hieroglyph of the verb "to be"

Everything feels like a fresh start

> The overcast sky
> doesn't help
> Rainsqualls will
> put out the sun

Are the bats better
Squeaking
Never turning right-side up
A whole society living upside down

At her table no one talks much about what they do in real life
The conversation is mainly   food   wine   travel

Dessert was outrageous
> *Roasted peaches in...   wasn't it...   in Costa...*
a marzipan...   the cream...   and

Sing in purple
     A song of want-a-pie
     A must play
     A delicious please

1

The pacific in the northwest isn't
     And beside there's rivalry there
     Among siblings

2

Little girl a strawberry soft inside this story
     Or an asparagus-mystery
     Unfolded up
     Into a pie
     (and twenty)

3

Into the goldenrod arounding the road
     Hope and a sparrow or two

4

She shrug/smiled me into putting on her white gloves
     Just washed and still drying in the parlor
     At first it was a problem
     Her having Yiddish, my not
     Then it wasn't
     Next day she left the house to live
     Happily-ever-after in the Home

5

Where else could I have found her or she me
     Any animal traveling through must swim
     And how _do_ porcupines make love
     In the counting house counting
     Snapping the book shut
     My fingers trapped between

nine, plus

.

The lights go out and there in the dark
(Of course, he cannot help himself)
stands a man perfectly formed

****

She wakes knowing she had been so
helpful: carried the woman
across the room
                    Later
she says *I think I*
am the one I
carried across

^^^

Red admiral butterflies are on the move:
sidewalk's a hop, skip, and jumping full up

Let us say we are all red monarchs
back flipping and cartwheeling in
capturing our lift from this
wake we will leave behind

∞∞

Paradoxical proximity to nonbeing:

A woman hands her book a book she won't open

±

Philosophy

She pushed into the toilet's
icy bottom to

try to remember the third
time she was told how

fast she slid (without gills) from
watery into

water.

Law

Picked up by a gust, she hits,
butt first, the western

wall of Philosophy. Whoa!
Up again and smacks

Law on its eastern flank. Stands
up and shouts: *I'm not*

I'm not.

Philosophy

Her hair brushes her friend's thick
corn-silk braid, jangling

jewels unbecoming what she
was, disappearing

she's smooth ribbons, unappears
into cord, into

a was.

A woman moves directly into the bedroom
  and suspects
    a blind flapping and a clock ticking,

pushes her face against the mirror. What is it?
  Sprocket holes
    in her optical track? Four players

sit in the dark room. If the fly-bee-bat lands on
  her, she wins.
    Johnnie-on-the-pony steals the bacon.

In the mirror, her eyes double on the goblet
  hurled and smashed
    hopped and tagged hide-scotch seek tic-tac-toe.

A few new figures have appeared, their backs to her
  sharp retorts,
    players that sprint through the woods, hands tied

behind their backs. If they hit a tree headfirst, they
  are so (dis)
    qualified. She hears cigarettes lit.

FIVE PLUS *CINQ* EQUALS
CINQ PLUS TWO PLUS THREE

Remembrance of time
wasted, walkway that leads to
first, a descending stairwell: witness it.

Is it now the girl
killed at the beginning of
this story appears in a yellow suit?

In a moment we'll
witness structural redun-
dance leaving traces of spirit about.

Blurring frames that give rue
(Could we ask for anything
more cinematic) to all accounts

(Can't be too many
around today.) The artist
of beautiful sleep glances backward at

the smitten camer-
a trailing obedience
behind her, coming-hither eye contact.

In a wilderness of mirrors

the white scar on her right thumb
speaks with the language of leaves

Wind-whipped she lets go of the road

sees a house where they would meet
what a spider would have seen

moves nearer when time became sky

her eyes inch-by-inch going
forward to the birds a-bath

snaps a rust-eaten ice window

charmed herself with ignoring
all that will be done and said

of wilderness and wind she and she

*

The night be   fore snow plows   every hour
    her ears are   her eyes with   as little

noise as pos   sible re   fraction is
    affected   by acts of   giving then

going e   very few   minutes con
    trasts in tex   ture and ar   ticula-

tion a salt   er then slush   tentative
    cars what in   strument is   joining in

*

The bus stopped, hovering again and over again, toward and into

*

I want to understand that a body
falling last night
didn't
she hear it

Says   Look
I'm looking at the blue-red-yellow in a white sea
But what does

she know
Says
I heard a loud thud last night
Says
I need to hear it again

*

And how did that prepare her for sunlight this morning when
the patch came off

Wakes one morning and the past's already here
at least the idea of it, nailing it
(looking at it from some serene remove).

The walks are November empty here.
In Tyson's Corner the window is cold
(even on the inside: a gray day).

Mechanic of an overarching pattern
the imagined butterfly that clings
(the kettle on the stove won't whistle).

Everything she sees: houses, statues, the sea
emerges from or vanishes in
the mist (that couple's) their cotton shirts.

That whistling kettle was a signal, listen:
He's wrinkled, she's starched (haphazard knot).
They do (not) really hear it at first.

You said *avoid Aristotle's three-part structure.* You said *write
sonnets.* Dilemma *primus*: sonnets in syllabics? *Secundus*:
let the title give the count-clue?

Last night responding to the silence I wrote these three lines:

> The lights go out and there in the dark
> (Of course, he cannot help himself)
> stands a man perfectly formed
>   (from "Letting One Go")

                    Use nouns and verbs. Dare I
say "perfectly" and "formed"?

                    Inside your dark-light you tell me
Every great poem has its flaw. No, I say.   Inside me,
I want to tell you, is the flawed one I don't know, the she/he
I call out to.

        Lately, Bill, I am at the beck and call
of images that keep creeping into the silence as
I write: your fingers folding and unfolding eyeglass frames,
playing in time to an urgent wit in six/eight, so
perfectly (There's that word again.) insightful. You take that
second, you smile. *Then maybe a walk, or after reading**
you start. *I'll prattle on but one more line*** Just one more line?

*Horace's *Satire I.vi*, translated by William Matthews
**and *Satire I.i*, translated by William Matthews

Four men in their forties disappear
  into the horizon
    in the forties.

Chopped meat's eleven letters won't fit
  into these ten spaces,
    but if it's ground?

Easier to fit in ground meat (beef?)
  than to understand why
    in the forties

it is possible that four men can
  vanish slowly into
    the horizon.

Ground meat kept sliding off the counter
  onto the black tile floor
    slipping away,

beneath the grass under leaden skies'
  soft saturating light.
    Youngest children,

displacers, should marry each other.
  Gone away growls and whines,
    she-saids they said.

Each sibling displaced by the next one
  for the rest of their lives.
    Who would have thought

Archimedes would keep popping up,
  that buoyancy should
    equal the weight

of the displaced water, whatever
  that means to child number
    first or second.

Every time an airplane touches down
  a computer boots up,
    a cake is born.

Her face has its geographic limits:
  she likes the look she sees,
    she looks alike.

In this elevator she rides up
  to the highest floor first.
    How, how Alice.

On one leg the hair grew a blond bush
  around her ankle,
    on the other

sharp and short black bristles up and down:
  Empire State and Chrysler,
    male and female.

Every other time an airplane takes
  off, her cell phone vibrates:
    Leave me a message.

At the seventy-fifth floor she sees
  soft sky all around her,
    at ninety-nine

a man walks out into his office.
  Alone now, she would say
    Take me with you.

Now what? The elevator's closed doors?
  She finger-fluffs her hair
    and waits. *Hello?*

nine, plus

Colophon

Design © Kstudio, New York.
Christiaan Kuypers, Noah Aronsson-Brown

Set in the following typefaces:

Scala, a serif font designed in the late
1980s by Martin Majoor.

DIN, a sans–serif font designed in the
early 1990s by Albert-Jan Pool.

Printed and bound by Town Crier, Ltd.,
Pella, IA, on Domtar Solutions Recycled
White 70lb Text, with a Xenon 80lb Cover.